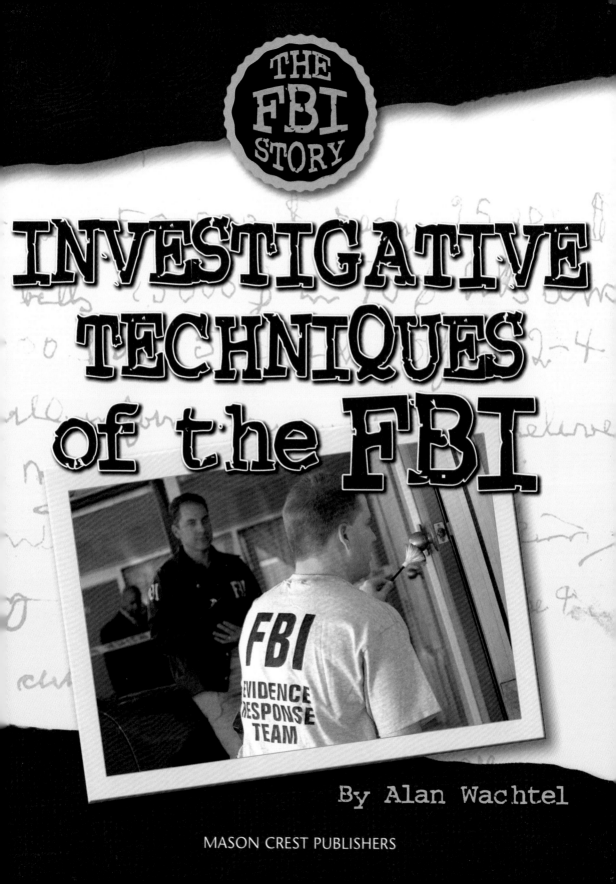

THE FBI STORY

INVESTIGATIVE TECHNIQUES of the FBI

By Alan Wachtel

MASON CREST PUBLISHERS

Produced in association with Water Buffalo Books.
Design by Westgraphix LLC.

MASON CREST PUBLISHERS INC.
370 Reed Road
Broomall, Pennsylvania 19008
(866) MCP-BOOK (toll free)
www.masoncrest.com

Printed in the United States of America

First Printing

9 8 7 6 5 4 3 2 1

Library of Congress Cataloging-in-Publication Data

Wachtel, Alan, 1968-
        Investigative techniques of the FBI / Alan Wachtel.
          p. cm. — (The FBI story)
        Includes bibliographical references and index.
        ISBN 978-1-4222-0572-3 (hardcover) — ISBN 978-1-4222-1379-7 (pbk.)
        1. United States. Federal Bureau of Investigation—Juvenile literature.
        2. Criminal investigation—United States—Juvenile literature. I. Title.
     HV8144.F43W335 2009
        363.250973—dc22   2009000591

Photo credits: © AP/Wide World Photos: 27, 37 (upper), 54; Berrien County Sherrif's
Department: 22, 23, 24 (left); © CORBIS: 5, 37 (lower), 56 (lower); © Courtesy of FBI:
cover (all), 1, 4, 6, 7, 8 (both), 9 (all), 10, 19 (all), 21, 24 (right), 25 (all), 29, 31, 44, 45, 53,
60, 62; © Getty Images: 28, 33, 51, 56 (upper); iStock Photos: 35; Courtesy of the Prints and
Photographs Division, Library of Congress: 32 (left); Used under license from Shutterstock
Inc. 11, 17 (both), 18, 20 (all), 32 (right), 36, 40, 42, 43 (both), 46, 49 (all); U.S. Department
of Defense: 12.

CONTENTS

CHAPTER 1 Solving Crimes Is Not Simple. 4

CHAPTER 2 At the Scene of the Crime. 12

CHAPTER 3 Boom and Bang. 22

CHAPTER 4 Fingerprints 32

CHAPTER 5 DNA Evidence 42

CHAPTER 6 Up Close to Suspects 48

Chronology. 57

Glossary 58

Further Reading 60

Internet Resources. 61

Notes. 62

Index 63

About the Author 64

CHAPTER 1 Solving Crimes Is Not Simple

On February 26, 1993, a huge explosion occurred in the underground parking garage of the World Trade Center. The blast killed six people and injured hundreds more. Some people thought that a power transformer had exploded. As soon as Dave Williams walked into the devastation, however, he knew what had caused the damage: a bomb. Williams was a member of the Explosives Unit of the Federal Bureau of Investigation (FBI). He was an expert on bombs and the damage they could do. Williams saw giant chunks of rubble that been blasted more than 700 feet (215 meters) away from the origin of the explosion. He

The 1993 bombing of the World Trade Center took place at around 17 minutes past noon on February 26. The explosion tore through five floors of the parking garage, creating a vast cave beneath the towers.

was confident that the explosion was no accident. He stood up among the various investigators and yelled, "Listen up everybody. My name is Dave Williams and I'm in charge here. From this point on, the FBI laboratory is coordinating this crime scene investigation."

Following the Trail

The investigators could not immediately figure out what explosive was used. They did, however, find large amounts of nitric acid and urea. Finding these chemicals at the bombing site was **evidence** that the bomb was homemade. Of the thousands of bombings they had investigated, it was only the second time they had seen this kind of bomb. Dave Williams and the other investigators knew that whoever had planted the giant bomb had to get it into the garage. From the type of damage they saw, they could tell which pieces had been close to the explosion.

They began looking for parts of a truck that could have carried the bomb. Soon, two investigators found a large piece

FBI investigators survey the damage caused by the explosion in the World Trade Center parking garage. The FBI joined forces with the New York Joint Terrorism Task Force to investigate the crime. The investigators' gut instincts told them this was a terrorist bomb— but they needed to find evidence.

Ramzi Yousef

Mohammad Salameh

Abdul Yasin

Mahmoud Abouhalima

Ahmed Ajaj

Nidal Ayyad

Eyad Ismoil

The World Trade Center bombers. The FBI used evidence found at the crime scene and evidence uncovered in their follow-up investigations to make a case against Salameh, Ayyad, Abouhalima, and Ajaj. Their investigative work would also lead them to the plot's mastermind, Ramzi Yousef, and Eyad Ismoil, who drove the van. Abdul Yasin, the seventh plotter, is still at large.

of the frame of the truck. The piece of truck frame was stamped with a vehicle identification number (VIN). This became the key piece of evidence that allowed the FBI to crack the case wide open.

The VIN led the FBI to Mohammed Salameh, who had rented the truck. Salameh had reported the truck stolen. When he tried to collect his deposit from the rental company, the FBI arrested him. Searching Salameh's belongings, the FBI linked him to Nidal Ayyad and Mahmud Abouhalima. These two men worked with Salameh to buy the chemicals for the bomb. After the media reported the details of the bombing and the arrests, the owner of a storage facility reported that he knew where the bombers kept their chemicals. Now, the agents had evidence that could connect the suspects to the crime scene.

As the investigation grew more complex, it uncovered new evidence and connections. Bomb-making pamphlets and videotapes led to another bomber, Ahmad Ajaj. Nidal Ayyad was linked to a letter claiming responsibility for the bombing. The FBI's DNA Analysis Unit found Nidal Ayyad's saliva on the envelope, and the FBI's Computer Analysis Response Team (CART) found a copy of the letter on his computer's hard drive. In addition, investigators found the building where the terrorists built the bomb. In the building, they found signs of the bomb chemicals in burns on the carpet and ceiling. The FBI used all of this evidence to make the case against the terrorists involved in the bombing.

The analysis of explosives, DNA, computers, and chemistry—these are just a few of the specialties of agents who work in the FBI Crime Lab. The investigative techniques used by these FBI agents made it possible to put away the 1993 World Trade Center bombers for life.

Crime Lab History

The FBI Crime Lab first opened on November 24, 1932. Before then, however, the FBI had already begun using **forensics** in its investigations.

The FBI Crime Lab was not the first. The first crime lab in the United States was run by Calvin Goddard. Goddard's lab, which opened in 1929, was part of the Northwestern University School of Law.

FBI agents were able to compare handwriting samples and bullets and analyze **blood types** in the FBI's first crime laboratory. In 1931, the FBI set up a national fingerprint file. In this photograph, a fingerprint expert analyzes fingerprint evidence.

This photograph shows Room 802 of the Old Southern Railway Building—the FBI's first crime laboratory. The lab's equipment included ultraviolet lights, for examining handwriting samples; a microscope, for looking at hairs and fibers; and a device that was said to help FBI agents examine gun barrels.

When the FBI's first Crime Lab opened, it had just one scientist—special agent Charles Appel.

The lab analyzed bullets, blood, and hairs and fibers. It also gave lie-detector tests. FBI director J. Edgar Hoover sent Agent Charles Appel to study at Goddard's crime lab. When Appel came back, he recommended that the FBI set up its own crime lab. He told Hoover, "The Bureau should be the central clearing house for all information needed in **criminological** investigation." Hoover appointed Appel to lead the founding of the FBI's Crime Lab. At first, the lab consisted of only one room and a few pieces of equipment. By 1939, the lab had added more agents, equipment for analyzing blood samples and other materials, and a lie-detector machine. One year later, it had grown into its own division of the FBI.

The lab continued to grow steadily over the next three decades. It was moved into bigger offices, and its technology was improved. The FBI Crime Lab's triumphs included figuring out how to see invisible ink used by German spies during

World War II. By the 1970s, the FBI Crime Lab was located in the J. Edgar Hoover Building—FBI headquarters—in Washington, D. C.

"Battlestar Galactica"

As successful as the FBI Crime Lab had become, it continually fell short in an important area. It did not have enough space for facilities that could keep evidence from becoming **contaminated**. In 1997, Congress approved funding for a new state-of-the-art building especially for the FBI Crime Lab. On April 25, 2003, the new FBI Crime Lab opened. Located in Quantico, Virginia, the new lab takes up about half a million square feet (46,500 sq m).

The new facility tripled the FBI Crime Lab's space. Most importantly, it was specially designed for the proper handling of evidence. The building has two separate air-handling systems—one for the offices and one for the

The FBI Crime Lab in Quantico, Virginia, takes delivery of about 600 pieces of evidence each day. To handle large pieces of evidence, the building has loading bays that can accept tractor-trailer trucks.

HELPING OTHER AGENCIES

As the premier crime lab in the United States, the FBI Crime Lab handles more than just FBI cases. Many law enforcement agencies lack resources for forensic investigation. Part of the FBI Crime Lab's job is to provide high-quality investigative services to these agencies for free. Smaller law enforcement agencies send evidence to the FBI Crime Lab for analysis. The FBI lab workers then prepare reports based on their work.

Another important way that the FBI Crime Lab helps other law enforcement agencies is by providing training. Every year, the FBI Crime Lab holds a series of courses on topics such as fingerprint detection, crime-scene photography, DNA analysis, crime-scene documentation, and investigation of explosions.

The courses are open to members of law enforcement agencies and the military. Like the FBI's lab work, its courses are also free.

labs themselves—to help make sure that evidence stays in good condition.

Once the evidence is in the building, it is analyzed by one or more of the FBI Crime Lab's 25 units. The Crime Lab includes units that specialize in Explosives, Trace Evidence, Firearms and Toolmarks, Chemistry and Biological Sciences, Fingerprints, and DNA analysis. With all the high-tech equipment that these units use—combined with the building's size and special design—a History Channel documentary reports that some people have nicknamed the new FBI Crime Lab building "Battlestar Galactica."

Members of law enforcement agencies from around the world can attend courses in investigative techniques offered by the FBI Crime Lab.

Other Techniques

Forensic techniques are not the FBI's only tools for investigating. Sometimes agents follow leads that can only be obtained from watching and following a suspect. In some cases, however, it is very hard to get close enough to criminals to see their crimes. In these cases, FBI agents sometimes go undercover. Undercover agents gain the trust of criminals by pretending to be on their side.

In other cases, the FBI has no idea who committed a crime. To help them figure out who the suspects might be, the FBI has a Behavioral Science Unit (BSU). The agents of this unit study the kind of person who is likely to commit a certain kind of crime. This kind of investigative activity is commonly known as *profiling*.

FAST FACTS

The FBI Crime Lab building has to be huge to handle its staff of about 700 scientists and technicians.

Sometimes FBI agents go low-tech and simply follow a suspect or even just watch the suspect's activities from a distance. Obtaining evidence from these investigative techniques—a form of surveillance—can take considerable time and patience.

CHAPTER 2 At the Scene of the Crime

Many crime scenes are shocking. Dead bodies, blown-up buildings, wrecked vehicles—all of these disturbing sights are signs of foul play. To know for sure what happened, however, FBI agents have to look very closely at the most disturbing crime scenes.

In many cases, the scene of a crime contains evidence

On April 19, 1995, a powerful bomb destroyed the Alfred P. Murrah Federal Building in Oklahoma City. The FBI agents first on the scene were witnesses to devastation—a building nearly reduced to rubble; cars burned to bare metal shells; and the terrible sight of many dead bodies and horribly injured people, including small children from a day care center. Working amid this chaos, FBI agents began their investigation.

The FBI's Trace Evidence Unit (TEU) examines the smallest pieces of evidence found at a crime scene. These traces can help investigators link suspects and victims during the commission of a crime. Shown here are enlarged images of the following trace samples found at crime scenes (counterclockwise from top): feathers, two different views of wood pieces and fibers, and a synthetic fiber shown under a special kind of light.

that tells the story of what happened. This evidence is sometimes hard to see. The Trace Evidence Unit (TEU) of the FBI Crime Lab analyzes tiny bits of material found at a crime scene. TEU agents look at human hair, animal hair, feathers, fibers, fabrics, rope, wood, soil, and glass from crime scenes. These "traces" can help connect a person to a crime. In addition to the TEU, the FBI also has a Chemistry Unit. From mysterious liquids, powders, and gases to pieces of metal, paint, and tape to deadly poisons, agents of the Chemistry Unit can analyze nearly any material found at a crime scene.

A Serial Killer On the Loose

From July 1979 to about May 1981, many people in Atlanta, Georgia, lived in constant fear. During this time, 30 young African Americans were murdered. The murders were grisly and shocking. The young victims were killed in different ways. By the time the FBI was called in, local investigators had found many hairs and fibers on the dead bodies. Some of them were unusual, greenish-yellow carpet fibers.

When a newspaper reported about the unusual fibers, the killer's tactics changed. The killer's previous victims were found fully clothed. After the report about the fibers, the dead bodies started showing up naked in the Chattahoochee River.

In response, the Atlanta police started watching the river. One night, they stopped Wayne Williams after he threw something off a bridge that crossed the river. Williams said he had thrown garbage into the river and told suspicious stories about where he was going. Two days later, the body of another murder victim washed up. In the hair of the victim was another greenish-yellow carpet fiber.

After this body washed up, investigators turned up the heat on Williams. In a search of his home, they took many fiber samples. They studied the samples and compared them to the samples from the murder victims. The unusual greenish-yellow carpet fibers on the victims matched carpet from Williams's house. In addition, other carpet fibers found on the victims matched rental cars

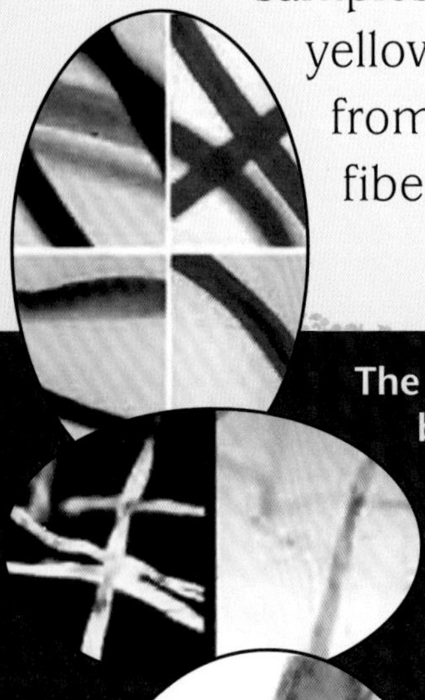

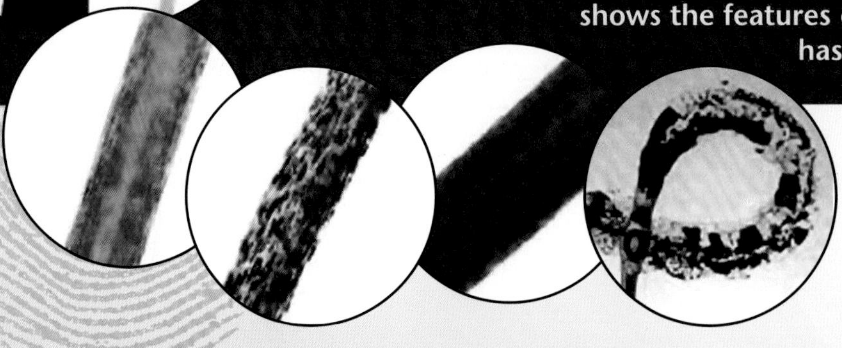

The FBI uses powerful microscopes to compare similar-looking bits of hair and fiber. In the samples shown here, differences are evident between different types of wool (top left) and different types of cotton (left). In the bottom row, the first three types of hair are (left to right) of European, African, and Asian origin. The last sample shows the features of a hair that has been burned.

Williams had used. Investigators discovered that the order in which these fibers were found matched the order in which Williams had rented the cars. Investigators even matched hairs found on some of the victims to hair from Williams's dog. These matches played a major role in the trial in which Williams was convicted and put away for life.

Hair-and-Fiber Analysis

Hair-and-fiber specialists are usually among the first experts to examine evidence. They look for human hairs, animal hairs, bits of rope, fibers from fabrics, and synthetic fibers. Just from looking at a human hair, experts can get a lot of information. A hair can tell them a person's race, whether the person has certain diseases, and whether the person drinks or uses drugs. If the root of the hair is attached, investigators can tell whether it came from a man or woman.

In many cases, after they have gathered hair and fiber samples from a suspect, they compare them to the hairs and fibers from the evidence. Hair-and-fiber specialists use powerful microscopes. **Compound microscopes** can make objects appear hundreds of times larger. They also use comparison microscopes.

A comparison microscope places the images of two compound microscopes side by side. Investigators check different characteristics of the samples and the evidence, such as how they curl, their texture, and their **diameter**. They can also use a piece of equipment called a microspectrophotometer to compare the colors of two samples. Using an infrared spectrophotometer, they can tell if two pieces of synthetic fiber are made of the same material.

If enough characteristics match, the investigators feel confident—but not absolutely sure—that the samples came from the same place. In David Fisher's book *Hard Evidence*, Agent Wayne Oakes says,

> It's extremely rare that we see hairs from two different people that are so close we can't tell them apart. . . . We can't testify that two hairs came from the same person. What we can say is that two hairs or two fibers are consistent in every measurable way and that it is highly likely that they came from the same source.

Telltale Green Spots

In the 1980s, a new and frightening type of crime made headlines. Back then, many **over-the-counter** medicines came in capsules and unsealed boxes. Some criminals opened the capsules, put poison inside, reassembled the capsules, and put the boxes on store shelves. Customers would buy the poisoned capsules, swallow them, and die. In 1986, Sue Smith took what she thought was Extra-Strength Excedrin and died of cyanide poisoning. As the media warned people against Excedrin, Stella Nickell called the police. She reported that her husband, Bruce, had died suddenly the week before—after taking Extra-Strength Excedrin. At first, doctors thought Bruce died of natural causes. Tests on a **preserved** sample of Bruce's blood showed that he, too, had died of cyanide poisoning. Investigators found two more bottles of poisoned Excedrin on store shelves.

Figuring out what killed Sue Smith and Bruce Nickell was the easy part. Finding out who did it took persistence, sharp eyes—and the skills of the FBI Chemistry Unit. Doug Martz, an FBI Chemistry Unit agent, examined the poisoned capsules. He noticed strange green material in the capsules that was not related to the cyanide. Martz isolated the green material and examined it with a **mass spectrometer**. It consisted of mostly salt and four other chemicals. Eventually, he and another agent learned that two of the chemicals were used mainly in **algae-cides**. Martz began looking at products used to kill algae in fish tanks. When he found a product called Algae Destroyer, he knew had made a big discovery. Algae Destroyer contained all four of the chemicals for which he was looking— and it was the exact color green of the mysterious material.

In the 1980s, the packaging of many over-the-counter medicines made it impossible to tell if someone had tampered with the medicine. Today, drug companies use "tamper proof" caps on bottles or seal capsules in foil packets.

Martz wrote a report about what he had found. An agent who read it put Martz's finding together with a detail he remembered: Stella Nickell had a large fish tank. Before long, the agent found the pet store that sold Algae Destroyer and a **mortar and pestle** belonging to Stella Nickell. It turned out that Nickell crushed the poison with the same mortar and pestle she

High-tech work in the FBI Crime Lab was combined with an FBI agent's low-tech observation skills to make a link between a chemical, a fish tank, and a murderer, Stella Nickell.

The FBI has a collection of different kinds of tape. It helps agents figure out where tape found at a crime scene was manufactured. Duct tape is so often used in crimes that some FBI investigators nickname it "crime tape."

had used to crush Algae Destroyer.

That was how the green material got into the poisoned capsules. At the same time, other evidence also pointed to Stella Nickell as the killer. It turned out that she killed Bruce so she could collect insurance money from his death. The insurance company would not pay based on a death from natural causes. She killed someone else to get Bruce's death reclassified as a murder—so she could collect insurance money. For these murders, Stella Nickell was sentenced to 99 years in jail.

Evidence Response Teams

To solve a crime, FBI agents follow a trail of evidence. In order make sure that all the evidence is gathered—and gathered correctly—the FBI has created Evidence Response Teams (ERTs). Beginning in 1995, each of the 56 FBI field offices had an ERT. As of 2003, the FBI had 130 ERTs and more than 1,000 agents. Among the biggest jobs for FBI ERTs was gathering evidence after the terrorist attacks of

Evidence Response Teams include members with many different skills and specializations. In the photo on the right, an ERT member dusts for fingerprints on a doorknob at a crime scene.

September 11, 2001. Fifty-two ERT teams spent nine months gathering evidence from the wreckage of the Twin Towers.

Becoming an ERT member requires an 80-hour basic course. After the basic course, ERT members take other course such as Blood Stain Pattern Analysis, Advanced **Latent** Fingerprints, Post Blast Investigation, Digital Diagramming, and Advanced Sketching. ERTs include photographers, sketch artists, evidence collectors/processors, bomb technicians, and computer specialists. They also include

FBI Underwater Search and Evidence Response Teams (USERTs) often have to deal with tough conditions as they search for evidence.

A dead body left at a crime scene is soon visited by flies and other insects that lay their eggs and feed on the dead tissue. Forensic entomologists can sometimes figure out when someone died by studying when the insects arrived on their body and by looking at the stages of the insects' life cycle.

Forensic anthropologists are often called "Bone Detectives." By examining the skeleton of a human, they can determine that person's gender, age range, height, racial makeup, and even what diseases or injuries the person may have had.

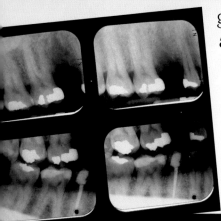

Dentists keep records of their patients' teeth, such as plaster casts and X-rays. Odontologists can sometimes identify a body found at a crime scene by matching the victim's teeth to a dentist's record.

surveyors, who measure and map land; forensic **anthropologists**; botanists, who study plants; odontologists, who study teeth; entomologists, who are experts on insects; and **arson** investigators, who determine whether a fire was set intentionally.

FBI Evidence Response Teams will follow a lead wherever it takes them, even underground or underwater. To find evidence underground, they use underground-penetrating radar. To find evidence underwater, they use **sonar** and special teams of scuba divers. Although ERTs have many high-tech tools, sometimes all they need to gather evidence are dogs. ERT members use specially trained dogs for tracking scents.

Many Uses of Chemistry

The FBI Chemistry Unit deals with a wide variety of cases. In some cases, the Chemistry Unit uses space-age equipment to defeat drug **smugglers**. Some drug smugglers know how to turn cocaine into a liquid and combine it with plastic. Neither dogs trained to smell drugs nor ordinary tests can find cocaine hidden in this way. The FBI's miniature ion spectrometer, however, can. The miniature ion spectrometer was originally developed to analyze the atmospheres of distant planets. The Chemistry Unit adapted it for crime fighting. It vacuums particles off an item and can tell within seconds whether cocaine is present.

FBI Human Scent Evidence Team bloodhounds are sent to help law enforcement operations around the United States search for bodies or kidnap victims.

Knowledge of chemistry can also help uncover a liar. The Chemistry Unit has taken part in many cases in which a criminal has sold a fake medicine. In one case, a criminal claimed that his homemade medicine could cure cancer. The criminal said the "medicine" contained ground-up diamonds and pearls, and he charged people with cancer thousands of dollars per bottle. Chemistry Unit agents examined the "medicine." They found no diamonds or pearls. All they found was a substance believed to be apple butter.

21

CHAPTER 3 Boom and Bang

In the late 1920s, Chicago, Illinois, was known for feuds between rival gangs. The gang murder of February 14, 1929—Valentine's Day—made headlines. Seven members of Bugs Moran's gang were gunned down in a garage. At the crime scene, investigators found more than 70 **cartridges** that they knew were fired from .45-caliber Thompson submachine guns. Ten months later, in St. Joseph, Michigan, a police officer pulled over a motorist for a traffic violation. The motorist shot the officer and sped away. Someone, however, got the gunman's license plate number. When police found the gunman's apartment and searched it, they discovered two .45-caliber Thompson submachine guns. To see if

Two sheriff deputies pose for a photograph wearing bullet-proof vests and holding two weapons, including a submachine gun, found at gunman Fred Burke's home.

Crime scientist Calvin H. Goddard examines a weapon to see whether it had been fired since it was last cleaned. Goddard's crime detection laboratory became the Chicago Police Department Crime Lab as a result of its work on what came to be known as the St. Valentine's Day Massacre.

these were the guns used in the St. Valentine's Day killing, police called in Dr. Calvin Goddard—the man who trained Agent Charles Appel, the first FBI Crime Lab agent. Goddard used a comparison microscope to show that the markings on the cartridges matched the guns. Based on Goddard's testimony, the gunman, Fred Burke, was put away for life.

Ballistic Techniques

The study of what happens in a gun as it is fired is called *ballistics*. The basic techniques of ballistics that the FBI uses today are the same they were in Goddard's time. Today, however, FBI agents have the benefits of decades of experience and modern technology. They are able to match bullets to the guns from which they were fired with great accuracy.

As soon as the Firearms and Toolmarks Unit receives a bullet found at a crime scene, they know in general what kind of gun they are looking for. Bullets come in different sizes, so only certain guns can fire them.

In the early days of ballistics, agents test fired guns into a long box stuffed with cotton (left). Today, the FBI Crime Lab has a special tank filled with water for test firing (above).

When investigators find a gun at the scene of a crime or on a suspect, then the work of matching the gun and the bullet begins. Firearms-and-Toolmarks agents need a sample bullet to which they can compare the bullet they found. To get the sample bullet, they must test fire the gun. An agent fires the gun through a metal tube and into an 8-foot- (2-m-) long tank of water. The bullet quickly slows down and sinks to the bottom of the tank, from where an agent can easily grab it with tongs.

Once the agents have the sample, they compare the markings on the sample to the markings on the evidence. The markings on a fired bullet come from the inside of the gun's barrel. Inside a gun barrel are spiral grooves. As the bullet travels through the gun barrel, the raised portions of the grooves, or lands, make tiny scratches on the bullet. Every type of gun barrel leaves its own type of tiny scratches. If the scratches on the bullet match the lands in a barrel, then the bullet was fired from that type of gun. That is helpful information, but the Firearms-and-Toolmarks agents can do even better: They can match a bullet to a specific gun. Each gun has a unique pattern of wear inside its barrel. If the marks on a bullet match this unique pattern, then the bullet was fired from that specific gun. If a person's gun can be connected to a bullet that killed someone, this can be used as evidence against the person. When the FBI Crime Lab finds that a bullet does not match someone's gun, this information can help defend an innocent person.

FAST FACTS
The FBI's reference collection of firearms includes about 6,000 guns. In the collection are weapons used by famous criminals such as John Dillinger and Alvin "Creepy" Karpis.

The markings made on a bullet by a gun's barrel (top) are like an individual "fingerprint" for that gun. A bullet from a crime scene (center) can be examined side by side with a bullet from a test firing of a particular gun (bottom) to see if the crime scene bullet and gun match up.

Something To Hide

Analyzing a toolmark is similar to analyzing a bullet. When a tool is used on an object, the marks that it leaves can be connected to the tool. FBI Crime Lab agents use microscopes to compare tools to objects on which they may have been used.

George Gwaltney was a California highway-patrol officer. In 1982, he reported finding Robin Bishop murdered by the side of a highway. As part of the investigation, detectives asked Gwaltney to turn in his gun, but Gwaltney said it had been stolen. When detectives searched Gwaltney's truck, they found the frame of his gun without the barrel. Without the barrel, they could not try to match the gun to the bullet that killed Bishop. Still, looking closely at the gun frame yielded evidence against Gwaltney. The frame had a mark on it that looked like it came from a gripping tool. Firearms-and-Toolmarks agent Jim Cadigan explains how he connected the damage on the gun frame to Gwaltney:

> Among Gwaltney's tools we found a pipe wrench with a broken tooth. I tested it on a piece of metal and it left a very similar looking mark. Using that mark for **orientation**, I was able to positively identify other marks found on the gun frame with marks made by other teeth on the pipe wrench. I could show exactly how the wrench had held the frame, and the broken tooth gave us the unique mark we needed to prove it had been held by this particular tool.

Gwaltney had lied about his gun being stolen, and the tool-mark evidence from his gun's frame showed that he had

The reconstructed remains of Pan Am Flight 103 are housed in an aircraft hangar in Farnborough, United Kingdom. After the disaster, investigators combed hundreds of square miles of Scottish countryside collecting fragments of the aircraft. Some pieces of evidence were no bigger than fingernails.

something to hide. Gwaltney was convicted of the murder and put away for 99 years.

Murder In the Sky

On December 21, 1988, Pan Am Flight 103 blew up in mid-air over Lockerbie, Scotland. All 259 people aboard were killed. Eleven people on the ground were also killed. Pieces of the plane, its cargo, and the bodies of its passengers spread over 845 square miles (2,200 sq kilometers) as they fell from the sky. Although the crime scene was in Scotland, the plane and many of the victims were American. The Explosives Unit of the FBI Crime Lab played a major role in the investigation.

The investigation proved that a bomb had caused the crash—and provided the clues that led to the capture of the bomber. Hundreds of detectives picked up every piece of the fallen plane that they could, recording where the pieces were found. They reassembled the pieces in an aircraft hangar. The

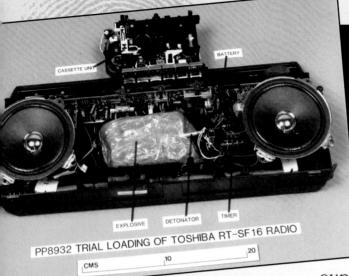

CASSETTE UNIT

BATTERY

EXPLOSIVE   DETONATOR   TIMER

PP8932 TRIAL LOADING OF TOSHIBA RT–SF16 RADIO

CMS   10   20

This photograph shows a mock-up of the Toshiba cassette player that was packed with explosives and placed inside a suitcase on Pan Am Flight 103. The mock-up was built as part of the investigation and used as evidence in the case.

investigators quickly found **residue** of an explosive called Semtex on a luggage container. They knew that Semtex is commonly used by terrorists. The Semtex residue told them that the bombing was most likely an act of terrorism. The piece of the luggage container also gave them important information. Records showed where the luggage was on the plane and what bags were near it. From this information, investigators guessed that the bomb was put on the plane at a stop in Frankfurt, Germany. As they picked up more pieces, they found fragments of Samsonite luggage and a Toshiba radio that showed direct damage by the bomb.

According to Tom Thurman, the top FBI agent working on the Pan Am Flight 103 bombing,

Explosive damage has very distinct look. Bomb fragments will have jagged edges and they might be coated with residue or soot. Depending on the force of the explosion, they'll probably be a little smaller than the debris resulting from a crash. If people know what to look for, bomb damage isn't hard to identify.

DANGER! LIVE BOMB!

One of the greatest dangers faced by Explosives Unit agents is coming face-to-face with a live bomb. Live bombs can still explode, so they must be approached with great caution. To make matters harder, agents do not have the opportunity to study many bombs before the bombs are used in crimes. Many bombs are homemade weapons known as improvised explosive devices (IEDs).

In 1980, a bomber planted a very complex homemade bomb in a Nevada hotel and casino. The bomb contained 1,000 pounds (450 kilograms) of dynamite and several **mechanisms** for setting it off. FBI agents X-rayed the bomb in an attempt to figure out how to disconnect its power source—the best way to disarm a bomb—but the wiring inside the bomb was very complicated. As time ran out, agents knew they had to act. They got all the people out of the building and tried to disrupt the big bomb with a smaller bomb that might disconnect the power source before it could set off the dynamite. It did not work. The giant bomb blew a five-story hole in the building.

Today, the FBI has a new tool for dealing with live bombs: robots. Agents operate robots such as the Andros V1A by remote control. The robot has cameras mounted on it to allow agents to see the bomb up close. Then, agents pick up the bomb with the robot's arms to move it away from people. Finally, the agents use the robot's special water-cannon system to disarm the bomb. The water tears the bomb open and separates its parts.

Equipment, including a remote control bomb disposal robot (far left), is unloaded from an FBI "bomb truck." The FBI bomb technicians were on standby in Washington, D.C., during the inauguration of President Barack Obama in January 2009.

It seemed that they knew everything except what they really needed to know—who put the bomb on the plane.

In early 1990, the Pan Am 103 bombing investigation broke wide open. Among the pieces gathered from the crash was a tiny piece of circuit board. It was, investigators believed, part of the timer that set off the bomb. One investigator thought he had seen that kind of timer in a bomb that the FBI had found in a case two years earlier. They looked at the older bomb, and, according to Thurman,

> We took the timer apart and examined it under a microscope. Bingo! . . . . Finally, we had something substantial that could lead us to the bomb maker. . . . We'd found the needle in the 845-square-mile haystack.

In the older bomb, the agents found the initials of the company that made the timer. The maker was a company from Switzerland that had sold timers to the Libyan government. Further investigation linked the clothing in which the bomb was wrapped to a Libyan agent, Abdel Basset Ali al-Megrahi. It took more than a decade, but eventually Libya admitted its role in the bombing, and al-Megrahi was given a life sentence for planting the bomb.

Bomb Maker Signatures

Bomb experts believe that each bomb maker builds his bombs in a specific way that can give him away. Bomb makers, they say, have a "signature." A bomb maker's signature can help investigators connect bombings that otherwise do not seem related. According to Explosives Unit agent Fred Smith,

This is a collection of components and tools used in the making of Improvised Explosive Devices (IEDs). This evidence is being examined by the Terrorist Explosive Device Analytical Center (TEDAC). TEDAC has received more than 24,000 IEDs since 2003. The IED material is examined for trace evidence and is used to make links between bomb makers and terrorist groups.

[W]hen a bomb has four or eight, whatever, points of construction that are the same as other bombs, it's appropriate to conclude that the same person made all those bombs or that they were made by someone following his instructions.

To assist investigators in solving bombing cases, the Explosives Unit has created the Explosives Reference Collection and the Bomb Reference File. The Explosives Reference Collection includes samples of items that can be used in building bombs. It includes items such as batteries, wires, timers, fireworks, fuses, and remote controls.

In addition, it includes catalogs and manuals that help investigators find out where bomb parts were made. The Bomb Reference File includes details of bomb designs and information about bombers themselves. The Explosives Unit's collections also include samples of bombs that have been found intact and pieces of bombs that have gone off. Before adding an intact bomb to the collection, agents make sure it is no longer able to explode. All of these reference tools help agents link a bomb to a specific person.

4 Fingerprints

When U.S. president John F. Kennedy was assassinated in Dallas, Texas, on November 22, 1963, the investigation began immediately. Within two hours police had found a rifle by a window of the Texas School Book Depository. On the rifle

On November 22, 1963, as President John F. Kennedy (in the back seat at left, next to his wife, Jacqueline Kennedy) waved at crowds from his limousine on a visit to Dallas, shots rang out from the Texas School Book Depository (above). Within hours, the FBI would be taking part in one of its most high-profile cases ever: Investigating the assassination of a U.S. president.

Presidential assassin Lee Harvey Oswald's rifle, bullets, and passport on display by the National Archives during the 25th anniversary of President John F. Kennedy's death.

was a print from the palm of Lee Harvey Oswald. In addition, the detectives found Oswald's fingerprints on a stack of cardboard boxes placed near the window. All of this evidence pointed toward Oswald as the assassin of the President, but it was not enough. Oswald worked in the building, so it was no surprise his fingerprints were around. The rifle may have been left there by someone who wanted to make it look as if Oswald was the shooter. To make a stronger case against Oswald, investigators had to show that Oswald had left those prints at about the time that President Kennedy was shot. The agents of the FBI's Latent Fingerprint Unit did just this.

Building a Case

Looking at the techniques that the detectives in Dallas used to find the fingerprints, the Latent Fingerprint agents at the FBI Crime Lab noticed something unusual. The Dallas detectives had found the fingerprints with **dusting powder**. The

Latent Fingerprint agents knew that it was very hard to take fingerprints off of cardboard. Cardboard absorbs finger-prints. They did experiments that showed that the dusting-powder technique would only find finger-prints made on card-board boxes that were less than three hours old. It followed that Oswald had been by the window at about the time Kennedy was shot.

FAST FACTS

In addition to tying suspects to crimes, FBI fingerprint experts also use their skills to help identi-fy the dead after terrorist attacks and disasters. The FBI was involved in identifying people who died in the terrorist attacks of September 11, 2001, and during Hurricane Katrina in 2006.

Unlike Any Other

Fingerprints are the patterns of ridges and valleys of skin on the tips of human fingers. Each person's fingerprints are unique. Even if two people look alike in every other way, their fingerprints will be different. Therefore, fingerprints can be used to identify people. The FBI created its first file of fin-gerprints for identification in 1924. To take fingerprints for identification, a person's fingertips are first coated in ink. Then, the inked fingertips are pressed one at a time with an even, rolling motion on a special form. The form has boxes for each finger on each hand. Today, fingerprints are also taken with a **digital scanner**. In 1933, the FBI began using latent fingerprints to help solve crimes.

A set of fingerprints from a person's right hand (the thumbprint is far left). Fingerprints contain different kinds of patterns—called loops, whorls, and arches. These patterns are used by fingerprint experts to identify individual prints.

Using fingerprints to solve a crime requires matching fingerprints taken from a suspect to fingerprints found at the scene of a crime. The fingerprints found at crime scenes are usually not, at first, visible. That is, they are latent fingerprints. Latent fingerprints are copies of the patterns on a person's fingers left on things a person handles. Hands sweat, and sweat contains salt, **amino acids**, and other chemicals. When a person touches an object, the fingers leave behind prints composed of these substances. In addition, fingerprints can also be made of the grease, food, dirt, and blood that people commonly get on their hands.

Finding Fingerprints

The Latent Fingerprint Unit of the FBI Crime Lab uses many methods for finding fingerprints. Until the 1970s, the Latent Fingerprint Unit used only two main techniques to find fingerprints: dusting powder and chemicals.

Dusting powder was used on smooth surfaces, such as glass and plastics. The powder sticks to the copy of the ridges on the fingertip and thus helps agents see the fingerprint against the background. When they find a print, they use special rubber tape to lift it off the surface. On **porous** surfaces, such as paper, cardboard, and wood, agents used a three-chemical process. First, they used iodine

When investigating a crime scene, agents spread powders of various colors on surfaces that criminals may have touched. Light-colored powders are used on dark surfaces, and dark-colored powders are used on light surfaces.

fumes, then ninhydrin, and, finally, silver nitrate. Each of these chemicals makes visible different substance that fingers leave behind when a person touches a surface. Iodine reacts with body fats and oils; ninhydrin reacts with amino acids from perspiration; and silver nitrate reacts with body salts. The order in which agents used the three chemicals was important. If the order was broken, then the next chemical would not work.

Lasers Push the Technology Forward

In the 1970s, fingerprint technology took off. One of the problems with using dusting powder and chemicals was that they damaged the evidence. In the mid-1970s, agents began examining evidence under **lasers** in the Crime Lab. The powerful light of a laser made it possible to see fingerprints not visible in ordinary light. Plus, the laser did no damage to the evidence. Eventually, FBI agents began bringing portable lasers to some crime scenes. In one case, they caught a kidnapper by shining a laser on the ceiling above the top shelf of his closet. The kidnapper tied up his young victims and hid them up in his closet. The agents used the portable laser to find a footprint that linked the suspect to a victim.

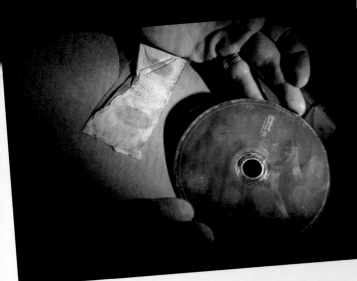

A laser (above) reveals fingerprints at a crime scene, while back at the Crime Lab (below) fingerprints on a CD are illuminated using cyanoacrylate, or superglue fuming.

The Superglue Solution

One problem with using lasers to find latent fingerprints is that lasers are expensive. One less expensive—and highly effective—method that the FBI uses to find latent fingerprints is superglue fuming. In 1979, a British police officer accidentally discovered that fumes from cyanoacrylate, or everyday superglue, stick to latent fingerprints. The fumes make the prints raised and easy to see. The FBI quickly began to make use of this discovery. Agents put small pieces of evidence in an airtight tank and then heat superglue so that the fumes flow over the evidence. Sometimes they add colored dyes or powders to make the prints even more visible.

To fume larger pieces of evidence, agents build an airtight tent around the evidence. Sometimes agents build tents around evidence so they can fume it at the scene of the crime. At some crime scenes, they have done this so they can try to find fingerprints on the skin of dead bodies.

Once latent fingerprints are found, they are photographed. These photographs are compared to fingerprints taken from suspects. One of the most difficult jobs of the Latent Fingerprint Unit is matching prints discovered on evidence to prints taken from suspects. In the past, agents spent a lot of time using microscopes to look very closely at the prints taken from evidence. Often, they only had an incomplete print from one finger, and they did not know which one it was. To match it to a suspect, they had to compare it to the

An Automated Fingerprint Identification System search can process its **database** of millions of prints in just a few minutes until it finds some close matches to a print found at a crime scene. An expert fingerprint analyst then examines the matches to find if one is a perfect match for the crime scene fingerprint.

prints from all 10 fingers of a suspect until they found a part that matched exactly.

Making use of latent prints was even harder when there was no clear suspect. After civil rights leader Martin Luther King, Jr., was assassinated in 1968, the FBI had a fingerprint from the murder weapon but no suspect. Using a description of the suspect and one of the first computerized fingerprint databases, they narrowed the list of known possible suspects from about 53,000 to 1,900. Agents began to compare the print from the gun to the prints of the 1,900 possible suspects.

According to Bobby Erwin, one of the agents involved in the investigation, "It was less than a needle in a

FINDING A NAZI'S FINGERPRINTS WITH A LASER

Valerian Trifa was an archbishop of the Romanian Orthodox Church of America. He had lived in the United States since the end of World War II. In 1975, the U.S. Department of Justice suspected that Trifa had been a member of the Iron Guard during the war. The Iron Guard was a pro-Nazi Germany political group in Romania. Although Trifa at first denied that he worked for the Nazis, evidence soon turned up against him.

In 1982, the government of West Germany found a postcard Trifa had written to a top Nazi official. The message on the card was a pledge of loyalty. To connect the card to Trifa, FBI agents checked it for fingerprints. The West German government would not allow them to use techniques that would damage the postcard. So, the agents used a technique that was new at the time: They looked at the card under a laser. The laser allowed them to find a thumbprint that matched Trifa's.

Trifa admitted that he had worked for the Nazis, and in 1982, in order to avoid being deported from the United States, he left the country on his own. After trying to find a country that would accept him, he settled in Portugal in 1984, where authorities also tried to have him removed from the country. He died in Portugal in 1987.

haystack, because we didn't even know if the needle was there." Luck, however, was on Erwin's side: The fifth set of prints he examined matched the print from the gun. It turned out that the print on the gun was made by James Earl Ray, an escaped con-vict. After he was caught, Ray was convicted of the murder and sen-tenced to 99 years in jail.

Today, the FBI's computerized fingerprint database is very important to its work. The FBI runs the Integrated Automated Fingerprint Identification Service (IAFIS). The IAFIS, which began working in 1999, is part of the Bureau's Criminal Justice Information Service (CJIS). The IAFIS contains fingerprints and criminal histories of more than 55 million people. Law enforcement agencies can give fingerprints they find to IAFIS. The fingerprint experts at IAFIS use their data-base to help find a match. IAFIS has helped cut the amount of time it takes to match latent fin-gerprints with suspects.

CRIMINAL PROFILING

Unlike fingerprinting, criminal profiling will not tell investigators who committed a crime. As part of an investigation, however, a profile, which is a kind of psychological or behavioral "portrait," can help lead investigators to that person. The FBI has two units that specialize in developing programs that use profiling and other techniques involving the study of human behavior. These are the Behavioral Science Unit (BSU) and the Behavioral Analysis Unit (BAU).

A criminal profile is produced using psychology (the scientific study of how the human mind works) and a thorough forensic investigation of the crime. The profiler will carefully examine the criminal's behavior at the crime scene and ask a variety of questions: What did the criminal do? How did he or she carry out the crime? Why did he or she carry out that crime? How might he or she do it again in the future? Understanding how and why can help investigators find the person who committed the crime.

Profiling is important because it can save agents lots of time during an investigation. After a crime has been committed, the investigating agency might receive thousands of tips from the public. There may also be thousands of pieces of evidence from the crime scene. The investigators may even have hundreds of possible suspects. To follow up on all these leads could take months, or even years—time in which the criminal might strike again. A profiler can help direct the search more successfully by building a profile of the type of person most likely to have committed the crime. This will help investigators eliminate suspects faster and focus on which pieces of evidence are most relevant.

The reality of profiling is not as simple as it is often portrayed in the movies or on TV shows like *Criminal Minds*, which is modeled after the FBI's Behavioral Analysis Unit. Real-life profilers can describe a "type" of person, but they cannot give that person a face or a name.

CHAPTER 5 DNA Evidence

On October 29, 2005, a father and son, David and Nathan Geiger, were attacked in their home on St. Thomas, one of the U.S. Virgin Islands. David, the father, was beaten to death. Nathan, the son, survived the attack but suffered traumatic injuries. Rennell Lettsome, the boyfriend of a woman who house sat for the Geigers, was charged with the crime. The house sitter was willing to testify against

A model of a DNA strand. In 1953, the scientists James D. Watson and Francis Crick discovered the structure of DNA—the genetic material that determines an organism's characteristics. Watson and Crick's discovery set the foundation for new investigative techniques.

DNA evidence can be collected from a splash of blood (above), from saliva on the neck of a bottle, from sweat, a hair, or even a tiny piece of skin. Except for identical twins, no two people have the same DNA.

Lettsome, but prosecutors also had even stronger evidence. Although Lettsome had set the Geigers' house on fire, investigators also found physical evidence against him. At the scene of the crime, they found blood that did not belong to either of the Geigers, and they also found water in a bottle from which someone had drunk. FBI nuclear DNA experts analyzed the blood and the water bottle. They found Rennell Lettsome's DNA, proving that he was at the scene of the crime.

DNA evidence also helped nail Garland Hall, a rapist and robber. On March 24, 2004, Hall broke into the home of an Eastern Michigan University student and raped her. A few hours later, he broke into the apartment of a University of Michigan student and tried to rape her. She successfully fought the attempted rape, but Hall stole her laptop computer and cell phone. Police found Hall with the computer and cell phone, but stronger evidence against him came from the first crime scene. Investigators found a hat that the victim said her attacker had been wearing. In the hat, they found a hair. FBI experts in mitochondrial DNA analysis matched the hair to Hall.

Identification Revolution

Like fingerprints, DNA provides the FBI with an accurate way of linking a person to a crime. Evidence found at the scenes of violent crimes often includes blood, hair, and bodily fluids from both victims and perpetrators.

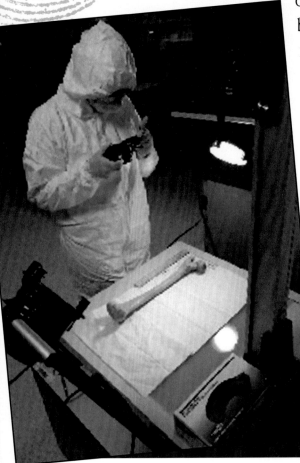

The FBI Crime Lab has two units that specialize in DNA analysis—DNAAU-1 and DNAAU-2. DNAAU-1 specializes in nuclear DNA analysis, while DNAAU-2 specializes in mito-

A DNAAU-2 biologist photographs a human femur (thigh bone) prior to mitochondrial DNA extraction. The bone is from an unidentified body. The DNA information will be fed into the National Missing Persons DNA Database (NMPDD).

chondrial DNA analysis. The two units examine DNA from different sources within human cells. Agents in DNAAU-1 look at DNA from a cell's nucleus, which is the part of the cell that contains the genes that control growth and reproduction. Agents in DNAAU-2 look at DNA from a cell's mitochondria, which are the parts of a cell that produce energy.

A person inherits nuclear DNA from both parents. Mitochondrial DNA, or mtDNA, comes only from the mother's side. As a result of this difference, nuclear DNA analysis can almost always point to a specific person. The only exceptions are identical twins, who inherit the same genes from both parents. Mitochondrial DNA

DATABASES

The FBI has a special unit just for DNA databases—the CODIS Unit. CODIS stands for Combined DNA Index System. The FBI began developing CODIS in 1990. A 1994 law granted the FBI the authority to set up a national DNA database (NDIS) to aid law enforcement. CODIS has six categories of DNA profiles: Convicted Offender, Forensic, Arrestees, Missing Persons, Unidentified Human Remains, and Biological Relatives of Missing Persons. By 2007, CODIS contained more than 5.3 million DNA profiles of convicted offenders and more than 200,000 forensic profiles.

In May 2001, the FBI's mitochondrial DNA analysis unit began setting up the National Missing Persons DNA Database (NMPDD). The NMPDD includes DNA profiles from certain categories of CODIS missing persons, relatives of missing persons, and unidentified dead bodies. The information in the database allows investigators to match DNA from a dead body with DNA from either a sample from a missing person or a sample from a missing person's mother, brother, or sister.

FAST FACTS

The FBI's nuclear DNA unit (DNAAU-1) is also responsible for the Bloodstain Pattern Analysis (BPA) Program. Agents look the size, shape, and location of bloodstains at crime scenes in order to figure out what happened.

A high-speed impact, such as that made by a bullet, creates a bloodstain pattern with many tiny drops of blood. The pattern can give investigators many clues as to the type of weapon used in the attack and the direction from which the impact came.

analysis can only point to a person from a specific mother.

In the field, the main difference between the two types of DNA analysis is the types of samples they examine. Agents can perform nuclear DNA analysis on samples of blood, saliva, semen, or other bodily fluids. Nuclear DNA analysis can get started with a tiny sample—as little as 50 molecules. Using a polymerase-chair-reaction (PCR) technique, agents can multiply their sample into a quantity of DNA large enough for analysis. Then, they use Short Tandem Repeat (STR) typing to develop a DNA profile, or DNA "fingerprint," of the person from which the sample came. STR typing looks at 13 different regions on a DNA molecule. Each of these regions can have different characteristics. With so many variables, the likelihood of two people having the same DNA profile is more than one billion to one.

Mitochondrial DNA analysis often begins with samples from bones, teeth, and hair. It can also be used on bodily-fluid evidence that has degraded because it is old or improperly stored.

DNA Uses

Forensic DNA analysis has many uses. According to the President's DNA Initiative Web site,

> . . . DNA evidence collected from a crime scene can implicate or eliminate a suspect, similar to the use of fingerprints. It also can analyze unidentified remains through comparisons with DNA from relatives. . . . DNA is also a powerful tool because when biological evidence from crime scenes is collected and stored properly, forensically valuable DNA can be found on evidence that may be decades old. Therefore, old cases that were previously thought unsolvable may contain valuable DNA evidence capable of identifying the perpetrator.

The FBI has used nuclear DNA analysis to solve murders, rapes, and bank robberies. Mitochondrial DNA analysis has helped the FBI in many cold cases. Cold cases are crimes that have been investigated but remain unsolved. The ability to analyze DNA from bones, hair, and teeth can give the FBI new leads in cases that have not been investigated in a long time. Mitochondrial DNA analysis can help solve missing-person cases by matching DNA from a long-dead body to DNA from a living relative.

6 Up Close to Suspects

Many FBI investigations deal with more than just evidence from crime scenes. In some cases, agents seek leads simply by watching and talking to suspects. In some dramatic cases, agents go undercover—that is, they pretend that they are criminals—in order to get close enough to suspects to get evidence directly from them or observe them committing crimes.

Surveillance

Surveillance simply means watching suspects to see what they do. The hard part of surveillance is making sure that suspects do not see the agents watching them. The FBI's Special Operations Division includes Special Surveillance Groups (SSGs). SSGs are teams of agents who work together to follow a suspect. Teamwork is key for members of SSGs. One of the main ways they make sure they are not seen is to use the "leapfrog" technique in order to avoid having the same agent following the suspect for long. An agent who has begun following a suspect will radio a description of the suspect to another agent stationed ahead. After a certain point, the first agent will stop following and another agent will pick up the trail. That way, the suspect will not see the same person following and grow

Special Surveillance Group agents carry different types of clothing so that the suspects they are following do not notice them. They might change from a business suit to jogging clothes, or even take a bicycle from their car's trunk so they can disguise themselves as a bicycle messenger.

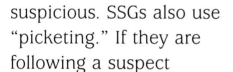

suspicious. SSGs also use "picketing." If they are following a suspect through a busy city, for example, the SSG may have agents stationed at many corners or subway stops. These agents are known as "pickets," and they are ready to pick up the trail of the suspect.

In addition to sharp eyes, SSG agents say that surveillance takes patience. According to an agent interviewed by Dina Temple-Raston for a National Public Radio story:

Every day you just get a little piece of the puzzle; you don't have to get the puzzle all in one day. . . . It's like something builds up to a very long story, if you will, like a soap opera more so as opposed to a cut-and-dry short story. . . . And you build on it every single day.

Even when following suspects does not immediately provide evidence to solve a case, surveillance can yield helpful information. An SSG agent described learning about the gangster John Gotti by following him: "You could just tell by his body language and the way people related to him whether he was in the middle of a crisis."

Lie Detectors

In FBI investigations, agents often interview many people. It is difficult for them to know who is telling the truth and who is lying to them. One investigative tool that helps them tell truthful people from liars is the polygraph machine. Also known as the lie detector, this machine has been used by the FBI since the 1930s. In 1978, the FBI Crime Lab set up a Polygraph Unit. In 2002, the Polygraph Unit became part of the FBI Security Division.

The name "lie detector" is misleading because the machine does not really tell true statements from lies. Instead, it measures the physical reactions a person has to certain questions. A modern polygraph has tubes and sensors that connect the body of the interviewee to a computer. The machine measures breathing rate, blood pressure, and perspiration from the fingertips as an investigator asks the interviewee questions. All of these measurements change with

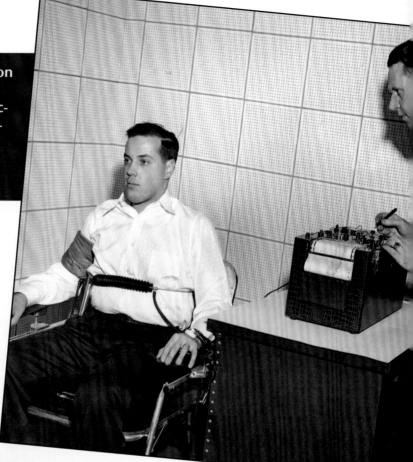

U.S. inventor John Larson demonstrates an early polygraph (or "lie detector") machine at Northwestern University, Evanston, Illinois, in the 1930s.

emotional stress. If a person is lying, polygraph users believe, the body will show stress even if it cannot easily be seen from the outside.

Polygraph tests are frequently controversial. Many people believe that the **physiological** changes the polygraph measures can be caused in a variety of ways, making the test unreliable. In 1938, even FBI Director J. Edgar Hoover spoke out against polygraph tests, after a polygraph test indicated that an innocent man was lying when he said that he did not commit a murder. In more recent times, polygraph tests are used to help establish the trustworthiness of a suspect or witness rather than to prove that a person is lying or telling the truth.

51

INVESTIGATING CYBER CRIME

To say that the development of computer technology has enhanced our lives would be an understatement. From wireless phones to high-definition TV, digital photography, online shopping, banking, and networking to high-tech medical treatment, computers make available more information, entertainment, and forms of communication than would have been thought possible only a few decades ago.

In the United States, government, the military, schools, and businesses rely heavily on getting information and communicating through vast computer networks. Taken as a whole, all the information that is communicated through these computer networks is known as *cyberspace*. Unfortunately, crime has taken its place alongside all the other incredible possibilities that have opened up in cyberspace.

The range of crimes committed in cyberspace is huge. These crimes include various types of scams or **fraud**. One common type of fraud occurs when a cyber thief illegally obtains and uses other people's credit card numbers. This kind of crime is one form of **identity theft**, in which purchases and electronic transfers of money are made by obtaining people's Social Security Numbers, credit card or bank account numbers, and other vital identifying information. Other scams include fake contests and emails that attempt to persuade potential victims to hand over money in get-rich-quick schemes.

This is to inform you of the release of money winnings to you. Your email was randomly selected as the winner and therefore you have been approved for a lump sum payout of $500,000.00.

To begin your lottery claim, please contact the processing company selected to process your winnings.

This email message tells you that you have been selected to win a huge amount of money in a drawing. But if it's a drawing for which you never registered, beware. It may be a lottery scam to get personal information that can be used to steal your identity.

The Internet has eliminated geographic boundaries and the need to travel to commit a crime. Tracing the origins of cyber crime can be very difficult, in part because the Internet makes it easier for crooks to conceal their identity and location.

Because it can be difficult for people to identify the source of cyber crime, the FBI encourages people to ignore email that asks them to share information that is private. The FBI also has several divisions and programs designed to help fight crimes committed in cyberspace. Probably the Bureau's best-known unit for combatting cyber cr███s its Cyber Division. The Cyber Division investigates all types of crimes that are committed with computers, including **hacking**, the spreading of computer viruses, the theft of **trade secrets**, and online fraud schemes.

In addition to the Cyber Division, the FBI has partnered with other organizations, such as the National White Collar Crime Center (NW3C). Together, the FBI and NW3C have created the Internet Crime Complaint Center (IC3). The IC3

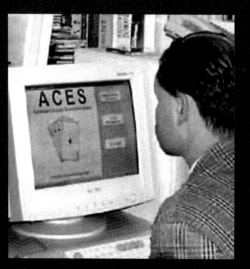

serves as a clearinghouse for investigating complaints and evidence of cyber crime. In addition to these operations, the FBI Cr███Lab has set up its Computer Analysis Response Team (CART). CART handles the search and seizure of computer evidence.

One of the most important tools used by the FBI's Computer Analysis Response Team (CART) is the Automated Computer Examination System (ACES). ACES helps agents in the field easily perform tests on computers and gather and record evidence taken from computers.

U.S. skaters (left to right) Tonya Harding (silver), Kristi Yamaguchi (gold), and Nancy Kerrigan (bronze) display their medals after the three won the top awards in the finals of the World Figure Skating Championships in Munich, Germany, on March 12, 1991. In 1994, Kerrigan was clubbed on the knee, making her unable to complete a competition in which she and Harding were entered. Harding was then implicated in a coverup during the investigation. Part of the drama of this episode revolved around Harding's former husband and his claim, which held up under a polygraph test, that Harding had been involved in the plot to attack Kerrigan prior to the 1994 Olympics.

A polygraph test helped investigators in this way as they got to the bottom of the attack on U.S. Olympic figure skater Nancy Kerrigan before the 1994 Olympics. Jeff Gillooly—the ex-husband of Tonya Harding, another top skater—was arrested in connection with the attack. Gillooly said that Harding was in on the plot to attack Kerrigan. When he passed a polygraph test, investigators began looking into whether Harding was involved. Harding later admitted that she knew who was behind the attack and hampered the FBI investigation. Gillooly was found guilty of planning the attack and went to jail.

Going Undercover

Sometimes FBI agents find that the most effective way to catch criminals is to join them—or, at least, to act like them and gain their trust. When FBI agents pretend to be criminals in order to gather evidence, they are said to be undercover. An undercover FBI agent takes on a false identity. The false identity allows the agent to get close to criminals and see how they work. In some cases, undercover agents may wear recording devices to record criminals planning crimes or talking about crimes they have committed in the past.

One of the most famous undercover FBI investigations began in 1976. That year special agent Joe Pistone took on the identity of Donnie Brasco. The man who called himself Donnie Brasco said he was a jewel thief. Slowly, Brasco worked his way into the Bonanno crime family, a major **Mafia** group that was involved in drug dealing. He got to know top Bonanno figures such as Benjamin "Lefty" Ruggiero and Domenic "Sonny Black" Napolitano. What began as a six-month assignment stretched into almost six years. Pistone had to learn the ways of the Mafia as he went along.

In a *National Geographic* interview, Pistone said,

> You have to know how things go down on the street. . . . You've got to know when to talk and when to keep your mouth shut. No one will tell you what to do. You have to have the mental toughness to handle it on your own.

While convincing the Bonanno family that he was one of them, Pistone identified many members of the Bonnano group and gathered evidence against them. At times, he recorded them talking about crimes they had committed or were planning. As Donnie Brasco, Pistone's life sometimes was in danger. At one point, a Bonanno member accused him of stealing from the group. "Donnie" convinced the gang leaders that he was innocent. If he had failed to convince them, they would have had him killed. Pistone's mission ended in 1981. The FBI pulled him out as Bonanno members began to turn on each other and bodies started to pile up. By that time, Pistone had gathered enough evidence to put away more than 100 Bonanno members.

A Vast Arsenal

The FBI's arsenal of investigative techniques is huge. It may include the most high-tech strategies, such as using laser, DNA, hair-and-fiber, and other forensic technologies to find out what clues lie below the surface of what most of us take for granted in our daily lives. Or it may consist of the same basic strategies that have been in use for decades, such as visual surveillance or going undercover. The common thread among all these techniques is persistence and a dedication to finding the truth.

In 1976, FBI agent Joe Pistone went under-cover, took the name Donnie Brasco, and infiltrated the mob. He is shown (above) in 1997 as an adviser to the motion picture *Donnie Brasco*, based on Pistone's autobio-graphical book of the same name. Pictured at right are the movie's stars: Johnny Depp as Pistone (left) and Al Pacino as mobster Benjamin "Lefty Guns" Ruggiero.

CHRONOLOGY

1924: The FBI creates its first file of fingerprints for identification.

1929: The first crime lab in the United States opens at Northwestern University.

1931: The FBI sets up a national fingerprint file.

1932: The FBI Crime Lab opens.

1933: The FBI begins using latent fingerprints to solve crimes.

1953: James D. Watson and Francis Crick discover the structure of DNA.

1963: FBI investigators find fingerprints that lead to the arrest of Lee Harvey Oswald for the assassination of President John F. Kennedy.

1968: FBI investigators find the fingerprints of James Earl Ray on the gun used to assassinate Martin Luther King, Jr.

1976: FBI Special Agent Joe Pistone goes undercover as Donnie Brasco to investigate the Bonanno crime family.

1978: The FBI Crime Lab sets up its first Polygraph Unit.

1979: The superglue-fuming method of detecting latent fingerprints is discovered.

1979–1981: FBI investigators find fiber evidence on the bodies of the victims of serial killer Wayne Williams.

1981: Pistone's undercover mission ends.

1982: FBI investigators use laser technology to find the fingerprint that helped identify Valerian Trifa as a Nazi war criminal.

1988: FBI agents investigate the terrorist bombing of Pan Am Flight 103.

1990: The FBI begins developing the Combined DNA Index System (CODIS).

1993: FBI agents investigate the terrorist bombing of the World Trade Center garage.

1994: Congress passes a law allowing the FBI to set up a national DNA database.

1997: The U. S. Congress approves funding for a new FBI Crime Lab.

1999: The FBI's Integrated Automated Fingerprint Identification Service (IAFIS) begins working.

2001: The FBI begins the National Missing Persons DNA Database (NMPDD).

Fifty-two FBI Evidence Response Teams (ERTs) begin gathering evidence from the wreckage at crash sites following the terrorist attacks of September 11, 2001.

2003: The new FBI Crime Lab opens in Quantico, VA.

2006: The Weapons of Mass Destruction Directorate is created to provide a central clearinghouse for information on weapons of mass destruction from various sources throughout the FBI.

GLOSSARY

algaecide—a substance used to kill algae, which is a plantlike organism that grows in water.

amino acids—the organic substances of which proteins are made.

anthropologists—scientists who study human beings in relation to their environment and culture.

arson—the crime of setting fire to property.

blood types—the groups into which blood is divided based on the presence of certain substances.

cartridge—a tube that contains the charge that a firearm ignites to propel a bullet.

compound microscope—a microscope that uses two or more double convex lenses in order to increase the magnification of objects.

contaminated—made impure or unfit for use.

criminological—having to do with the study of crime.

database—a computer system for organizing information.

diameter—the distance across the center of an object.

digital scanner—an electronic device that creates a computer image of a surface.

dusting powder—powder spread on objects by detectives to help make latent fingerprints visible.

evidence—material used to uncover truth or to prove guilt.

forensics—the study of physical evidence or information, often related to a crime.

fraud—using tricks or lies to get another person's money or property.

hacking—entering a computer without permission.

identity theft—taking the identity of another person, which often includes buying goods on credit using the victim's name and never repaying the debt.

laser—a device that creates a beam of electromagnetic radiation that can result in a very bright light.

latent—existing but not able to be seen without some substance or technique applied to make it visible.

Mafia—name for the network of Italian-American crime organizations. The term "Mafia" has also been applied to organized crime networks run by other ethnic groups.

mass spectrometer—a machine that identifies the chemicals out of which a sample is made by separating its gaseous ions according to their weights and charges.

mechanism—a set of parts that are made to work together, such as the parts of a machine.

mortar and pestle—a set of tools used for grinding or pounding consisting of a vessel (a mortar) and a clublike tool (a pestle).

orientation—the setting of a position to which other things can be related.

over-the-counter—available for sale without a prescription, usually in stores.

physiological—having to do with the body.

porous—having spaces or holes within a substance.

preserved—kept in an original state and free from decay.

residue—the substance that is left over after a process, such as an explosion.

smugglers—criminals who sneak goods into places where those goods are prohibited.

sonar—a method of locating an object in which sound waves are reflected off of the object.

trade secrets—secret formulas or processes that businesses use to make products.

FURTHER READING

Bell, Suzanne. *Drugs, Poisons, and Chemistry*. New York: Facts on File, 2008.

Beres, D. B., and Anna Prokos. *Dusting and DNA*. New York: Scholastic, 2008.

Cooper, Chris. *Forensic Science*. New York: DK Children, 2008.

Ford, Jean. *Explosives and Arson Investigation*. Broomall, PA: Mason Crest Publishers, 2005.

Hueske, Edward. *Firearms and Fingerprints*. New York: Facts on File, 2008.

Rainis, Kenneth G. *Fingerprints: Crime-Solving Science Experiments*. Berkeley Heights, NJ: Enslow Publishing, 2006.

DVD
The History Channel. *FBI's Crime Lab*. A&E Home Video, 2006.

INTERNET RESOURCES

http://www.dna.gov/case_studies/

The President's DNA Initiative Web site includes case studies of how DNA evidence has been used. From the capture of the North Carolina "Night Stalker" to stories of how DNA evidence has been used to set the innocent free to a series of stories that shows how DNA evidence could have been used to prevent crimes, this site shows how DNA analysis has changed FBI investigations.

http://www.fbi.gov/hq/cjisd/cjis.htm

The FBI Criminal Justice Information Service Web site features a special "All About Fingerprints" section. Click on "Taking Legible Fingerprints" for pictures and descriptions of the main fingerprint types plus a short video showing the proper way to take fingerprints from a suspect.

http://www.fbi.gov/hq/lab/labhome.htm

The Web site of the FBI Laboratory Services division gives an overview of the range of services offered at the FBI Crime Lab. Click on the names of the Crime Lab units to learn about their jobs and resources.

http://www.fbi.gov/kids/6th12th/investigates/investigates.htm

The FBI Investigates . . . A Strange Flashlight walks you through an FBI investigation of an attempted bombing. Follow the case from discovery of the evidence through the laboratory results. Be sure to click on the "How Did They Do That?" boxes to learn about the investigative techniques used in the case.

Chapter 1

Page 5: "Listen up everybody. My name . . .": David Fisher, *Hard Evidence: How Detectives Inside the FBI's Sci-Crime Lab Have Helped Solve Some of America's Toughest Cases*, New York: Simon & Schuster, 1995, p. 78.
Page 8: "The Bureau should be the . . .": Fisher, *Hard Evidence*, p. 17.

Chapter 2

Page 16: "It's extremely rare that we see . . . .": Fisher, *Hard Evidence*, p. 103.

Chapter 3

Page 26: "Among Gwaltney's tools we found . . .": Fisher, *Hard Evidence*, p. 256.
Page 28: "Explosive damage has a very distinct look. . . .": Fisher, *Hard Evidence*, p. 68.
Page 30: "We took the timer apart . . .": Fisher, *Hard Evidence*, p. 72.
Page 31: "[W]hen a bomb had four . . .": Fisher, *Hard Evidence*, p. 85.

Chapter 4

Page 39: "It was less than a needle . . .": Fisher, *Hard Evidence*, p. 140.

Chapter 5

Page 47: ". . . DNA evidence collected from a crime scene . . .": "About Forensic DNA," http://www.dna.gov/basics/.

Chapter 6

Page 50: "Every day you just get a little piece . . .": Dina Temple-Raston, "FBI Surveillance Team Reveals Tricks of the Trade," *NPR.com*, July 5, 2008, http://www.npr.org/templates/story/story.php?storyId=92207687.
Page 50: "You could just tell by his body . . .": Temple-Raston, "FBI Surveillance Team Reveals Tricks of the Trade."
Page 55: "You have to know how things . . .": Stefan Lovgren, "FBI Agent 'Donnie Brasco' Recalls Life in the Mafia," *National Geographic News*, June 10, 2005, http://news.nationalgeographic.com/news/2005/06/0610_050610_tv_mafia.html.

INDEX

Numbers in **bold italics** refer to captions.

Abouhalima, Mahmud, 6
Ajaj, Ahmad, 6
al-Megrahi, Abdel Basset Ali, 30
Appel, Charles, 8, 23
Automated Computer Examination System (ACES), *53*
Ayyad, Nidal, 6–7

ballistic investigation techniques, 23–25
Behavioral Analysis Unit (BAU), 41
Behavioral Science Unit (BSU), 11, 41
Bishop, Robin, 26
Bloodstain Pattern Analysis (BPA) Program, 46
Bomb Reference File, 31
Burke, Fred, *22*, 23

Cadigan, Jim, 26
Chemistry Unit, 13, 16–17, 21
Combined DNA Index System (CODIS), 45
Computer Analysis Response Team (CART), 7, 53
Crime Lab, 7, 11, 13, 25, 50
  and DNA analysis units, 44–47
  history of the, 7–10
  and training, 10
crime scene investigations, 12–21
Criminal Justice Information Service (CJIS), 40

Criminal Minds (TV show), *41*
cyber crime, 52–53

Dillinger, John, 25
DNA evidence, 7, 42–47
DNAUU-1 unit, 44–45, 46
DNAUU-2 unit, 44–45
drug smuggling, 21

Erwin, Bobby, 39–40
Evidence Response Teams (ERTs), 18–20
Explosives Reference Collection, 31
Explosives Unit, 4–5, 27–29, 31

Federal Bureau of Investigation (FBI)
  and ballistic investigation techniques, 23–25
  Chemistry Unit, 13, 16–17, 21
  and cooperation with other agencies, 5, 10, 53
  Crime Lab, 7–10, 11, 13, 25, 44–45, 50
  and crime scene investigations, 12–21
  and databases, *38*, 40, *44*, 45
  and fingerprint investigations, *7*, 32–39
  firearm reference collection, 25
  and hair-and-fiber analysis, 13–16
  and training, 10, 19
fingerprint investigations, *7*, 32–39
  and lasers, 36–37, 39

and superglue fuming, 37–38
Firearms and Toolmarks Unit, 23–27
Fisher, David, 16

Geiger, David and Nathan, 42–43
Goddard, Calvin, 7–8, 23
Gwaltney, George, 26–27

hair-and-fiber analysis, 13–16
Hall, Garland, 43–44
Hard Evidence (Fisher), 16
Hoover, J. Edgar, 8, 51

identity theft, 52
Integrated Automated Fingerprint Identification System (IAFIS), *38*, 40
Internet Crime Complaint Center (IC3), 53

Kennedy, John F., 32–34
King, Martin Luther, Jr., 39–40

Larson, John, *51*
lasers, 36–37, 39
  See also fingerprint investigations
Latent Fingerprint Unit, 33–40
Lettsome, Rennell, 42–43
lie detectors. *See* polygraph machines

Martz, Doug, 16–17
medicine tampering, 16–18
mitochondrial DNA. *See* DNA evidence

Moran, Bugs, 22–23

Napolitano, Domenic
("Sonny Black"), 55
National DNA Database
(NDIS), 45
National Missing Persons
DNA Database
(NMPDD), **44**, 45
National White Collar
Crime Center
(NW3C), 53
Nickell, Bruce, 16–18
Nickell, Stella, 16–18

Oakes, Wayne, 16
Oswald, Lee Harvey,
33–34

Pan Am Flight 103,
27–28, 30
Pistone, Joe (Donnie
Brasco), 55–56
polygraph machines,
50–51, 54
profiling, 11, 41

Ray, James Earl, 40
Ruggiero, Benjamin
("Lefty"), 55, **56**

Salameh, Mohammed, 6
Smith, Fred, 30
Smith, Sue, 16–17
Special Surveillance
Groups (SSGs), 48–50
St. Valentine's Day
Massacre, 22–23
superglue fuming, 37–38
See also fingerprint
investigations

Terrorist Explosive Device
Analytical Center
(TEDAC), **31**
Thurman, Tom, 28, 30
Trace Evidence Unit
(TEU), 13
Trifa, Valerian, 39

undercover investigations,
11, 48, 54–56
Underwater Search and
Evidence Response
Teams (USERTs),
19, 20

Williams, Dave, 4–5
Williams, Wayne, 13–15
World Trade Center
bombing, 4–7

About the Author

Alan Wachtel has been editing and writing educational books since 2001. He maintains an air of mystery that may or may not have any basis in fact.